The Wonder of Stones

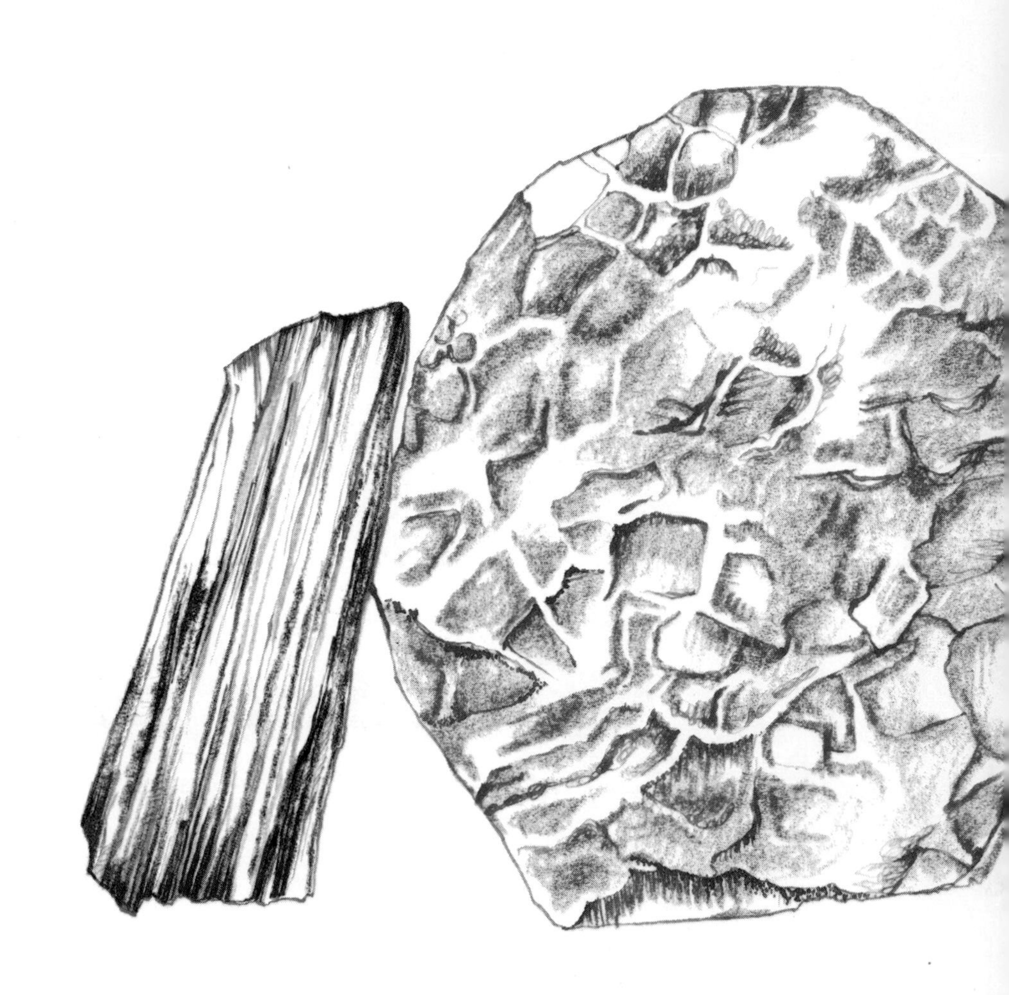

The Wonder of Stones

By Roma Gans

Illustrated by

Joan Berg

Thomas Y. Crowell Company / New York

LET'S-READ-AND-FIND-OUT BOOKS

Special Adviser: *DR. ROMA GANS*, Professor Emeritus of Childhood Education, Teachers College, Columbia University.
Editor: *DR. FRANKLYN M. BRANLEY*, Coordinator of Educational Services, American Museum—Hayden Planetarium, consultant on science in elementary education.

A Tree Is a Plant
How a Seed Grows
Seeds by Wind and Water
Down Come the Leaves
The Wonder of Stones
Big Tracks, Little Tracks
Animals in Winter
Starfish
Sandpipers
Birds Eat and Eat and Eat
Fireflies in the Night
Where the Brook Begins
The Clean Brook
Snow Is Falling
What Makes a Shadow?
Air Is All Around You
Rain and Hail
Upstairs and Downstairs
My Five Senses
Look at Your Eyes
My Hands
Find Out by Touching
Follow Your Nose
In the Night
The Listening Walk
How Many Teeth?
The Moon Seems to Change
What Makes Day and Night
The Sun: Our Nearest Star
The Big Dipper
Rockets and Satellites
What the Moon Is Like

 Manufactured in the United States of America. Library of Congress Catalog Card No. 63-15087.

1 2 3 4 5 6 7 8 9 10

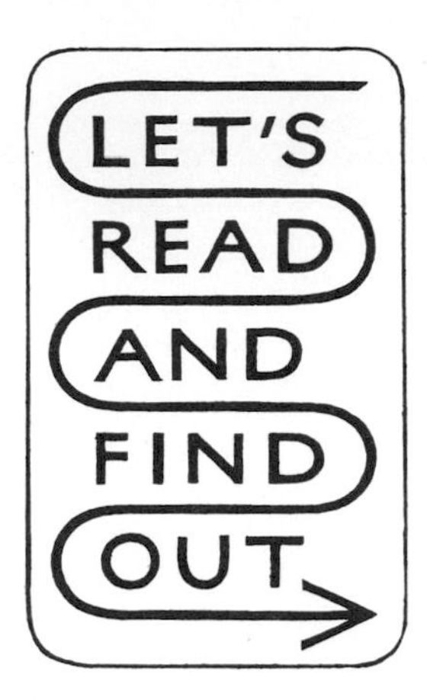

The Wonder of Stones

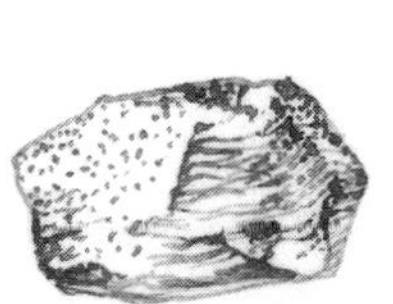

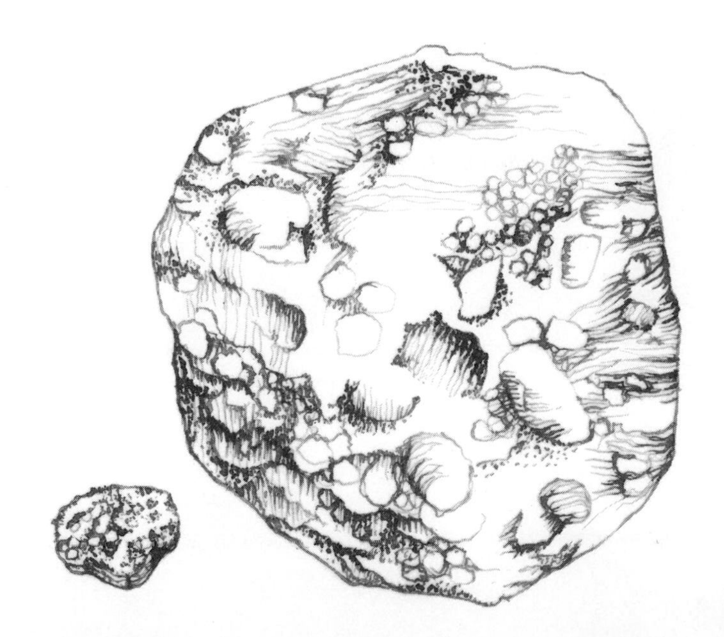

Big stones and little stones,
Flat stones and round stones,
White stones and pink stones,
Dull stones and shiny stones,
Most of them old stones.
There are only a few new stones.

New stones are made by volcanoes.
Melted rock comes out of the volcano.
The melted rock cools
and new rocks are formed.

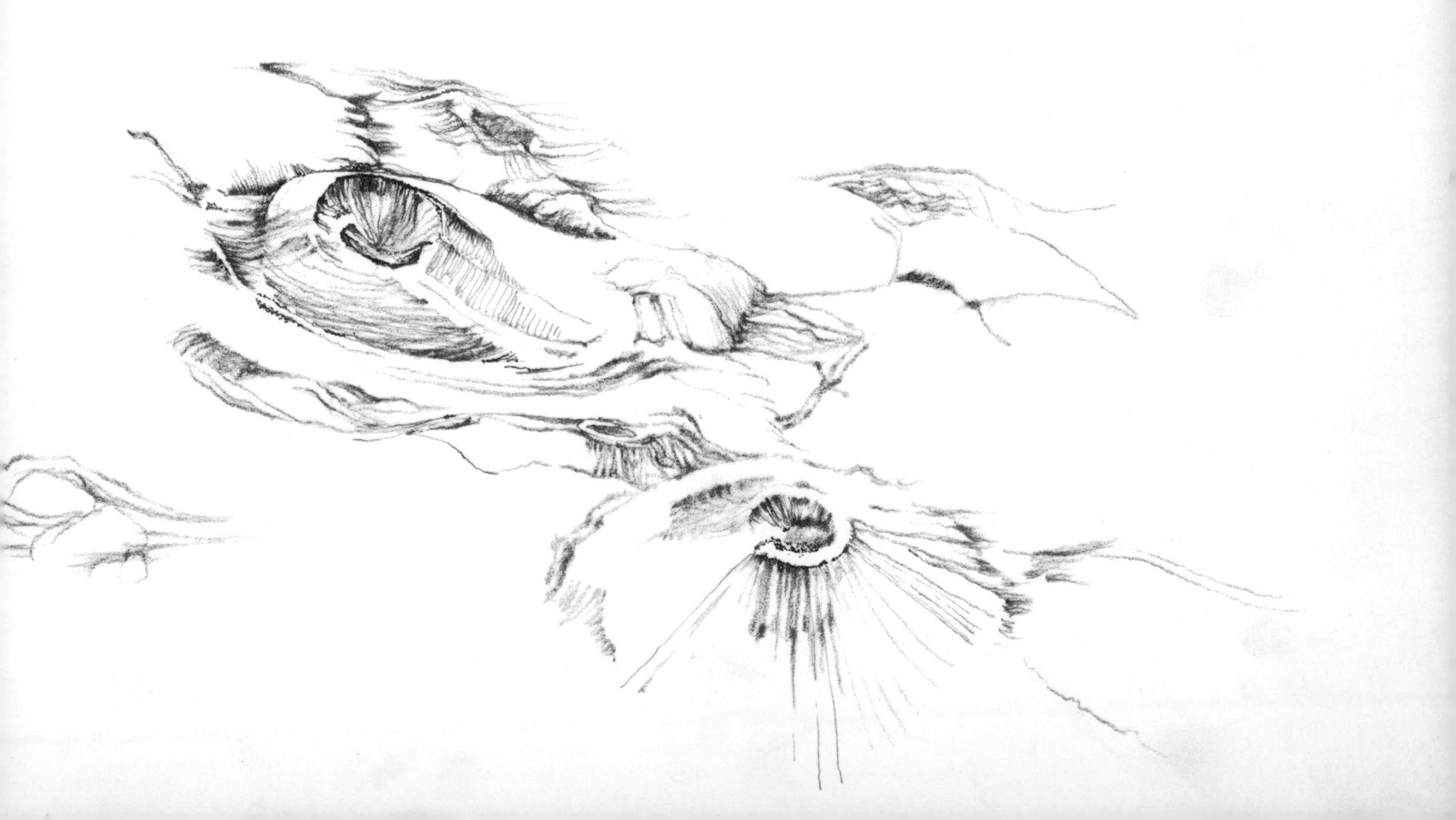

New stones are made under the sea.
But most stones are very, very old.
The stones are made of sand
and clay, bones and shells.
Sometimes you can see
the shells in the rocks.

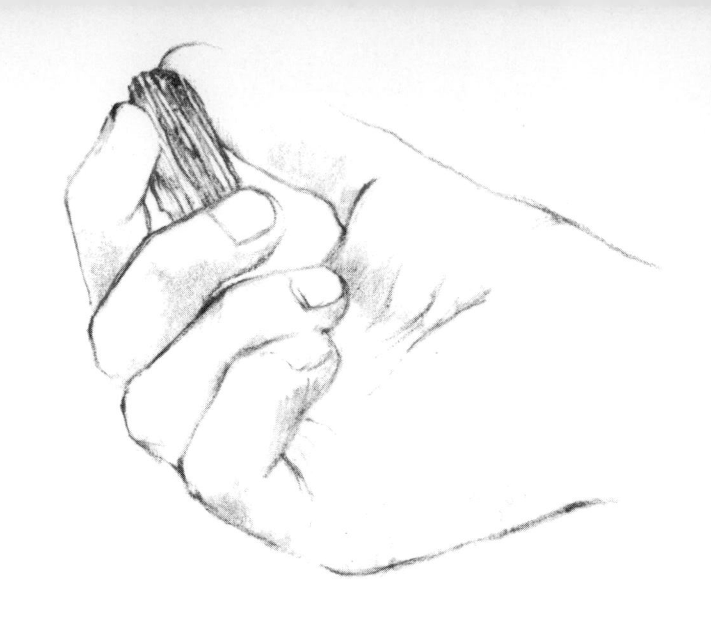

Hold a stone in your hand.
The stone in your hand may be
more than a hundred years old.

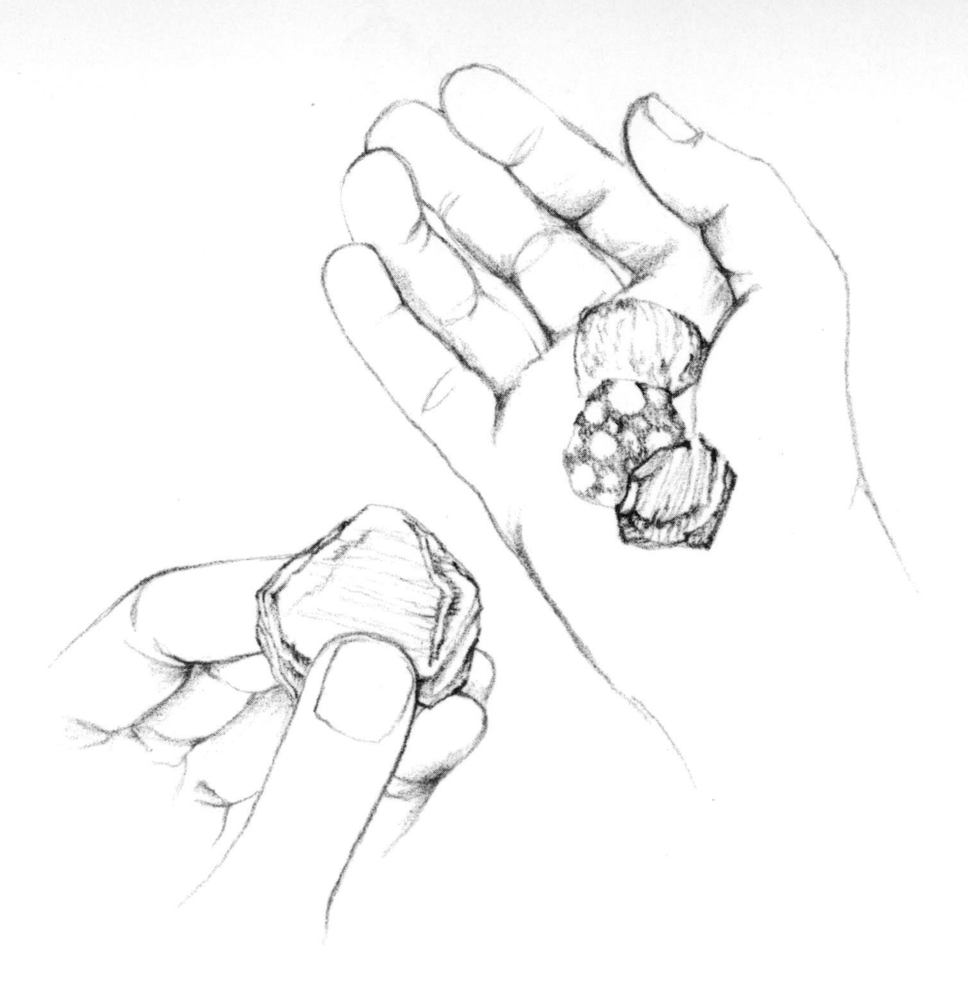

It may be more than a thousand years old.
It may be more than a million years old.
It may be more than a billion years old.

The stone in your hand may be
older than trees,
older than cities,
older than houses and churches.

The stone in your hand may be
millions or billions of years old.

Flat stones and round stones,
Little stones and big stones.
Some stones are so big that
they must be broken and moved.
When new roads are built
through mountains of granite
the stones must be broken
and taken away.
When a workman breaks
a big piece of granite

Just think:

He sees what no one has ever seen before.
No sunlight ever shone on it.
No air ever touched the inside of that stone.
No soil ever fell on it.

He is the first person to see
the inside of that stone.
After millions of years, this piece
of granite is open for us to see.

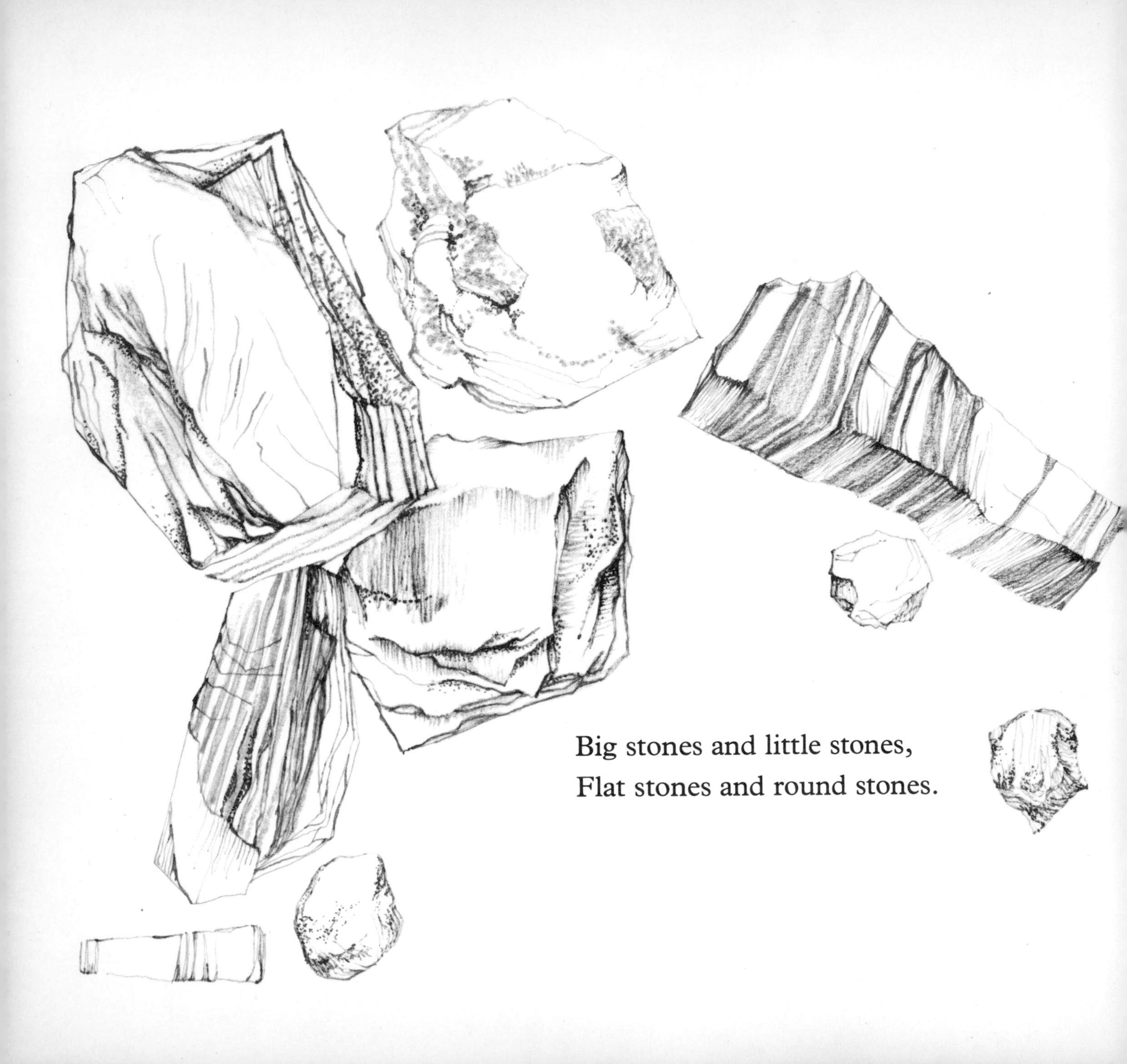

Big stones and little stones,
Flat stones and round stones.

How were stones made ?

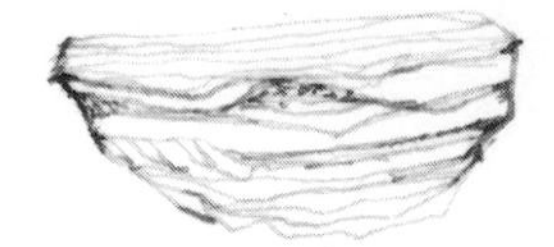

The inside of the earth is very hot, hot enough to melt rocks.
Melted rock pushed into cracks in the crust of the earth.
The hot melted rock cooled and cooled and became very hard.

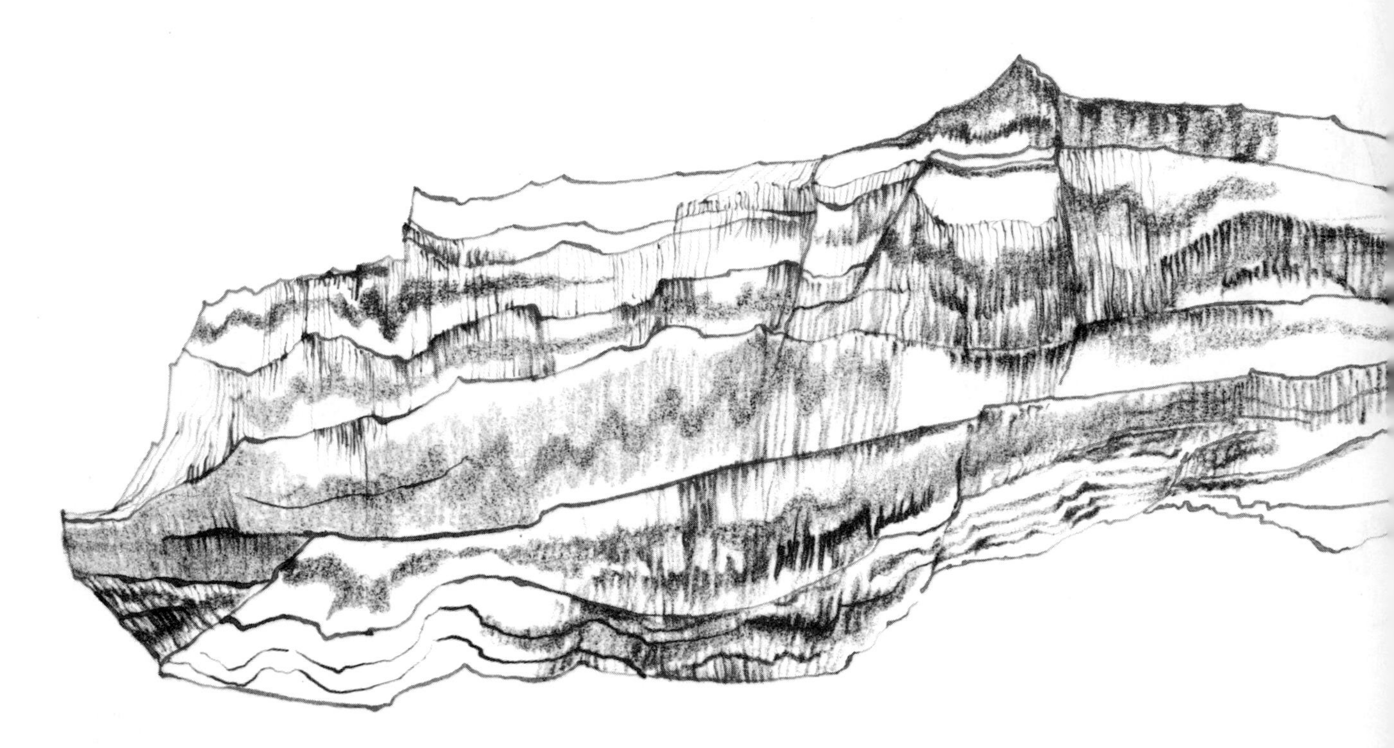

Sometimes the rock cooled slowly.
Then many particles joined together little by little.
They became large colored parts in the rock.
You can see them.

Sometimes the hot melted rock cooled quickly.
It cooled so quickly that only a few particles joined together.
They became small colored parts in the rock.

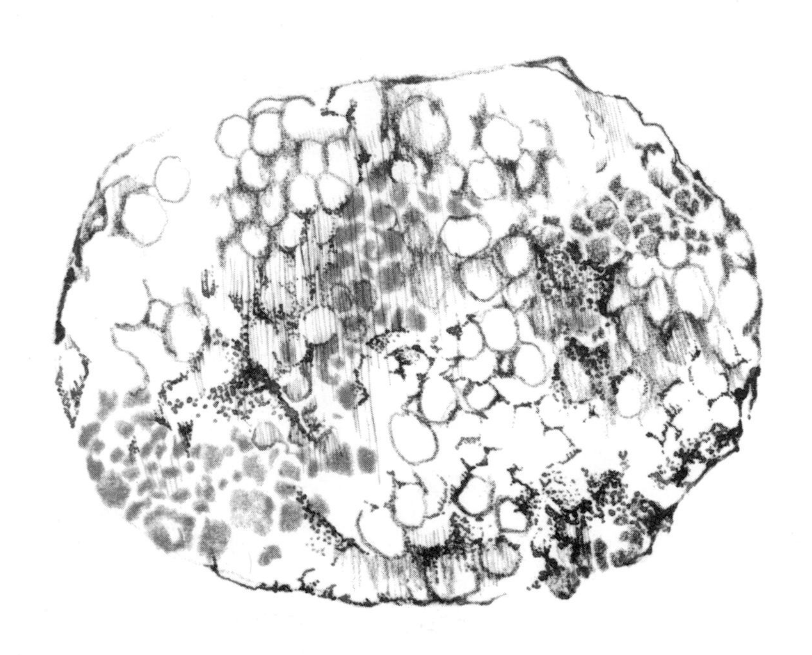

You can see them, too.
Some of the colored parts
are black like pepper.

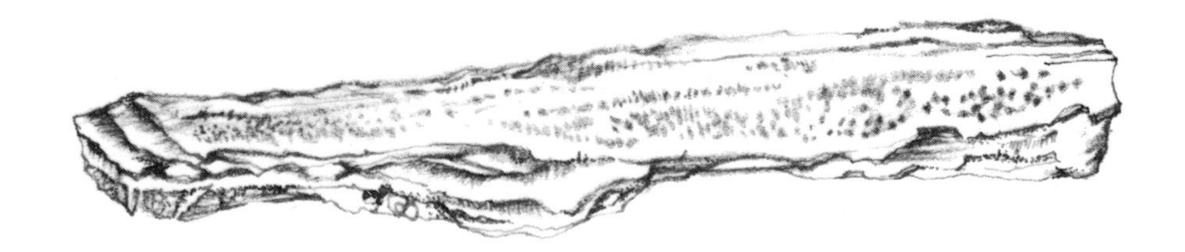

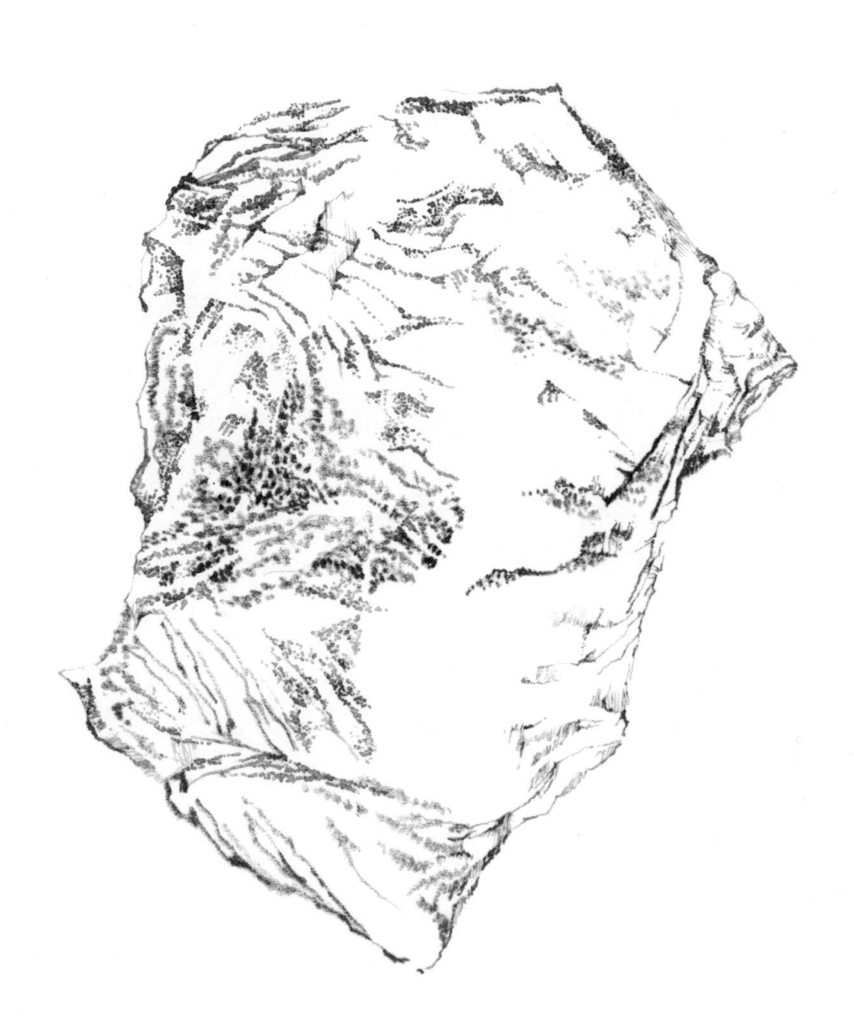

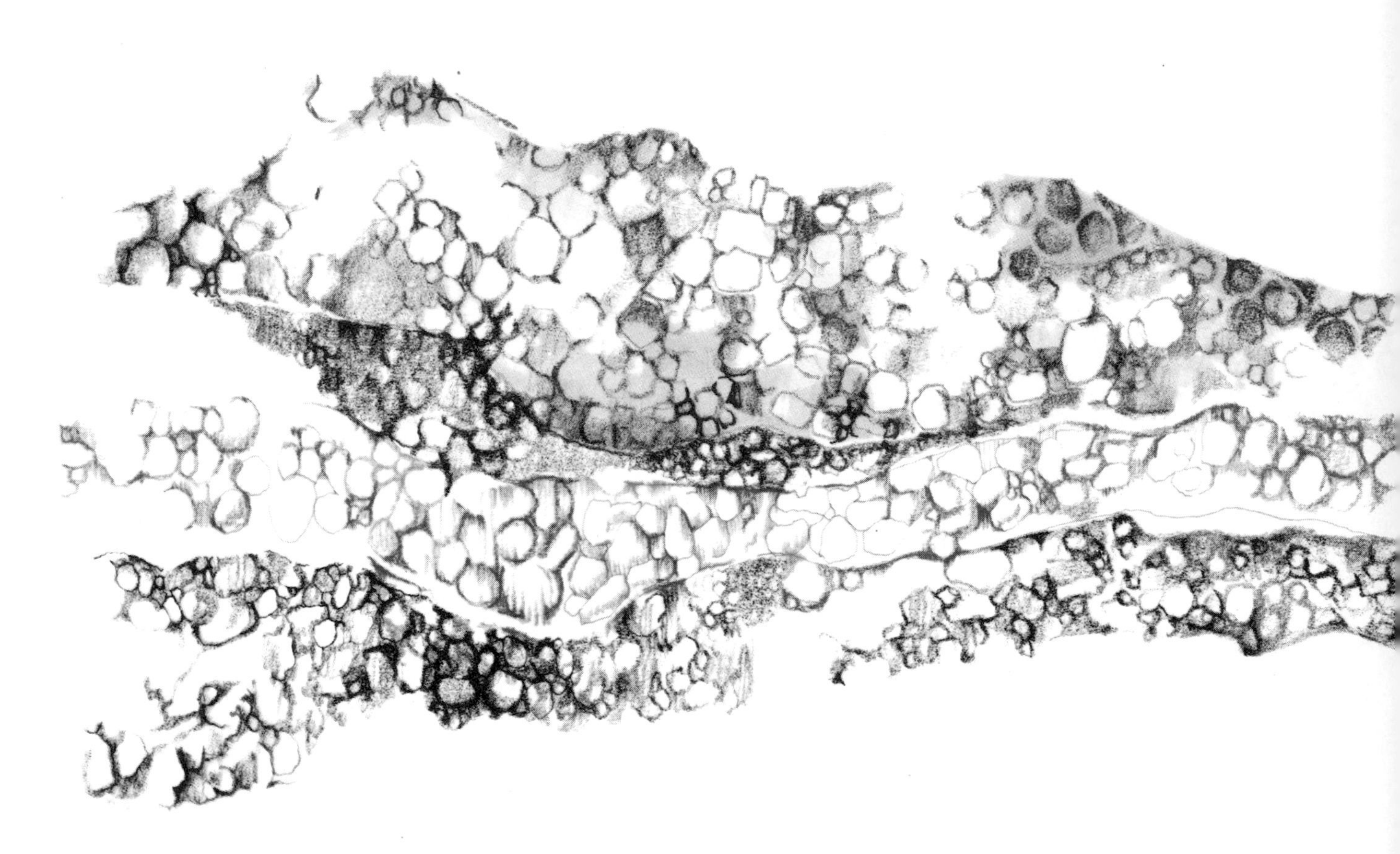

Some of the colored parts are blue.

Sometimes you will find blue and white,
pink and black all in one stone.
Sometimes you will find only one color.

Not all stones are made of melted rock.
Some stones are made of layers of sand.
Long ago grains of sand were carried by water.
The water dropped the sand,
making layer after layer.
After years and years the sand
became hard and made stones.
Stones of clay were made this way, too.
Water carried the grains of clay
and dropped them in layers.
The layers hardened and became stones.
Sometimes you can see the layers.
Sometimes you can feel the sand.
Many of these stones were made
thousands and thousands of years ago.
New stones of sand and clay are being made today
under lakes and seas and rivers.

You can find out about stones yourself.
You can make your own collection.

Look for stones when you go on trips.

Look for stones in
your own back yard.

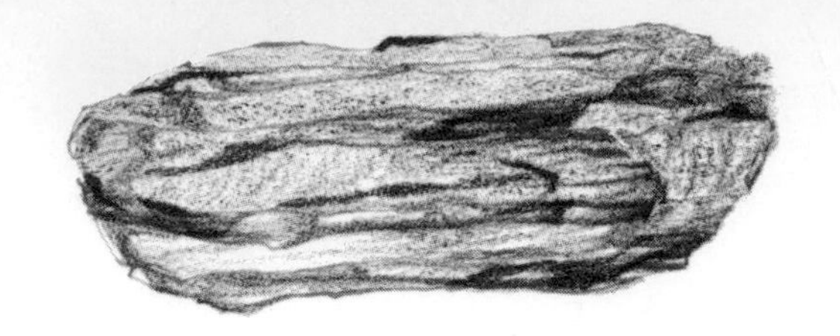

Look for layers in your stones.

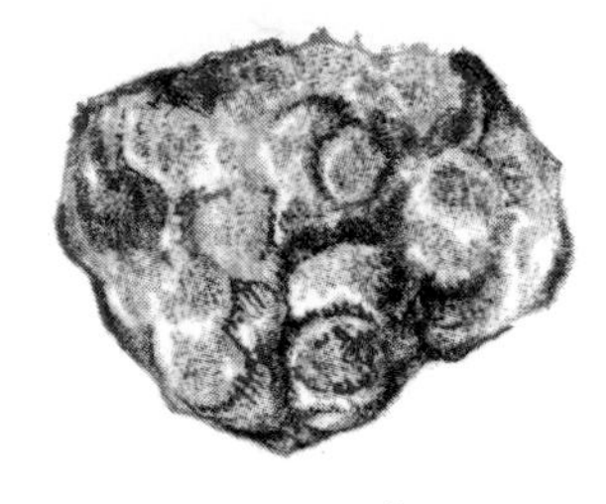

Look for colors in your stones.

Big stones and little stones,

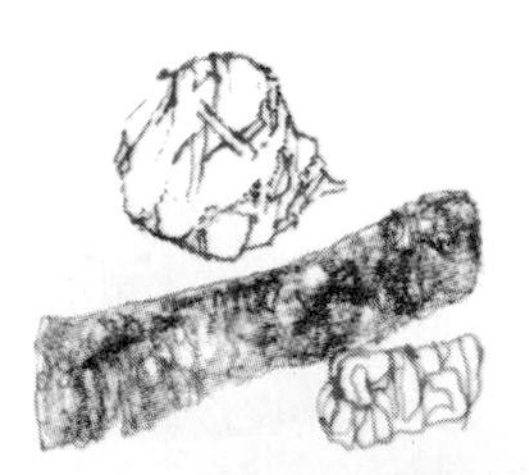

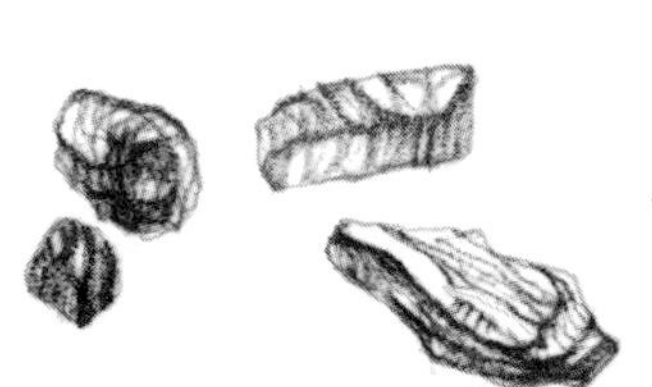

Flat stones
and round stones,

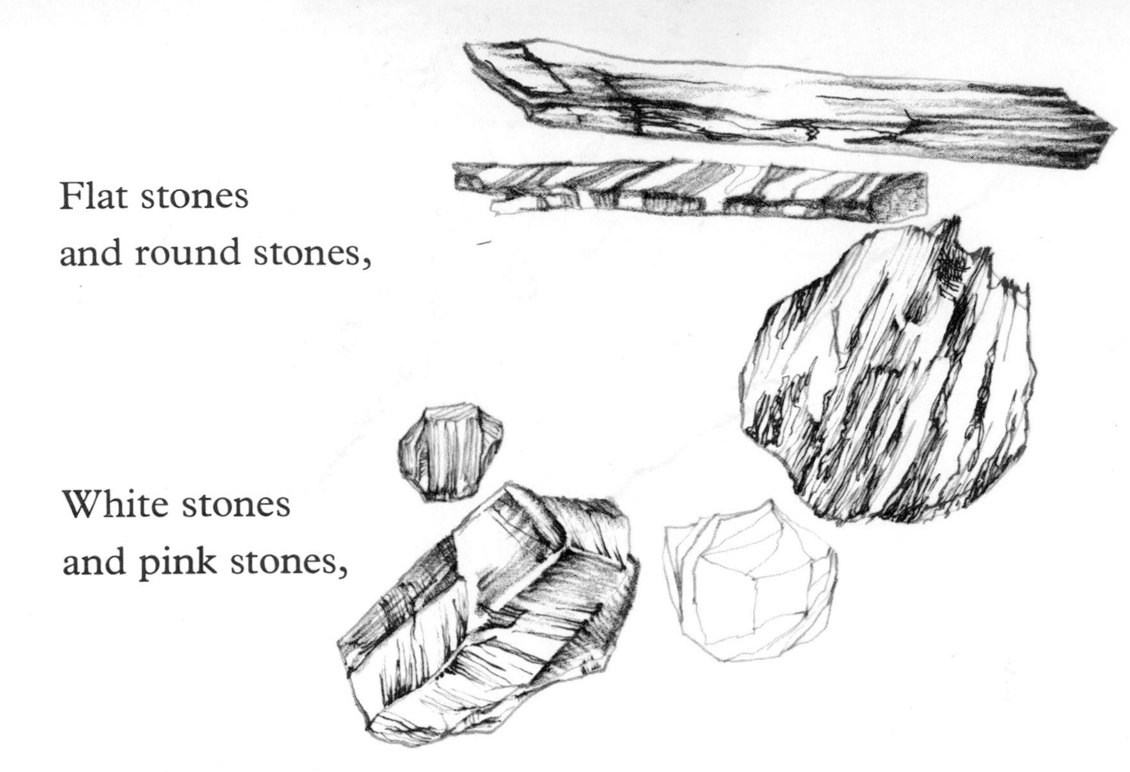

White stones
and pink stones,

Dull stones and shiny stones,
Most of them old stones,

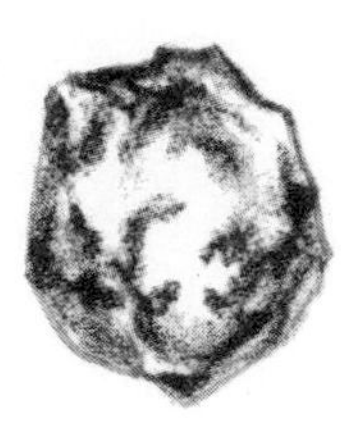

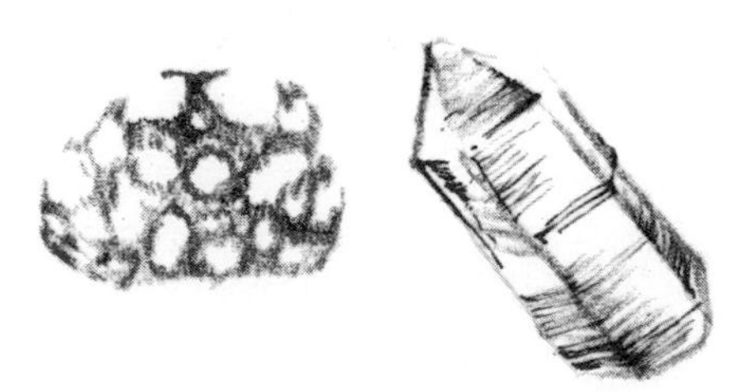

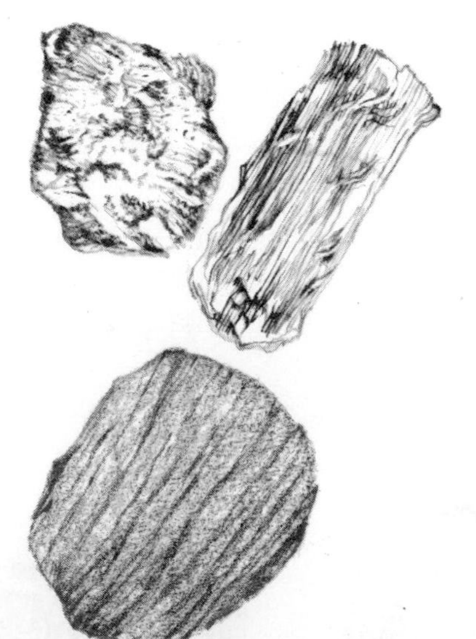

Older than
towns and cities,

Older than
houses and churches.

Stones may be thousands
or millions or billions of years old.

And here they are in your collection.

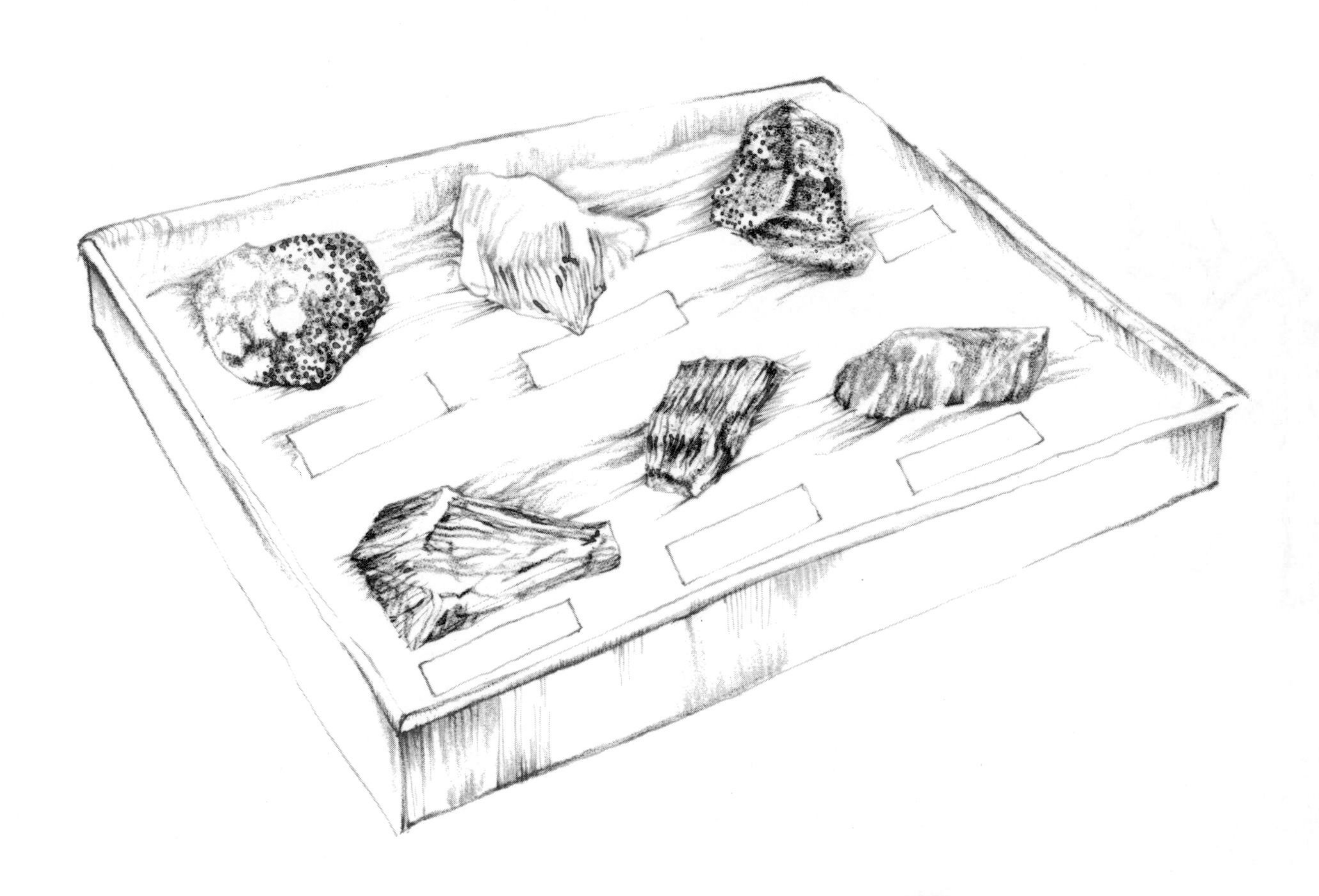

ABOUT THE AUTHOR

Roma Gans has called children "enlightened, excited citizens." She believes in the fundamental theory that children are eager to learn. Place the right teacher in the classroom with them, put good up-to-date books, magazines, and other materials within their reach, and children themselves whet their own intellectual curiosity.

Dr. Gans received her B.S., M.A., and Ph.D. at Teachers College, Columbia University. She began her work in the educational field in the public schools of the Middle West as a teacher, supervisor, and then superintendent of schools. She is Professor Emeritus of Childhood Education at Teachers College, Columbia University, and lectures extensively throughout this country and Canada. All of her research has been in the field of reading. Dr. Gans is the author of *Reading Is Fun*, *Guiding Children's Reading Through Experiences*, *Critical Reading in the Intermediate Grades*, and, just recently, *Common Sense in Teaching Reading*. With Dr. Franklyn M. Branley, she is supervising and editing the Let's-Read-and-Find-Out books.

ABOUT THE ILLUSTRATOR

Joan Berg had her first New York one-woman show of her paintings and drawings in October 1962. Her illustrations have appeared not only in books but in a multitude of periodicals. Those magazines include *Harper's Bazaar*, *Mademoiselle*, *Glamour*, *The Reporter*, and *Seventeen*. In her spare time she works with cerebral palsied children, attends the opera and the theater, takes modern dance lessons, and hikes.

Miss Berg was graduated from Sophie Newcomb College of Tulane University and received her M.F.A. degree from Yale University. She lives in New York City.